HEY MAN, WE JUST TALKIN'

Daily Conversations With Young Men

Dedrick J. Sims

**HEY MAN,
WE JUST TALKIN'**
Daily Conversations With Young Men

Creative Director
Jasmine C. Cole

Photographer
Kearrious Reed

Publishing & Managing Editor
Lisa J. Petros

Published by
One-L Group, a subsidiary of From the
Heart International Educational Services

Printed by BookMasters, in the United States of America,
Second printed edition 2022

One-L Group Publishing
From the Heart
Po Box 151569
Arlington, TX 76015

Book Contributors

I'd like to thank the following men who added tremendous value to this book. Their powerful words and perspectives will have a great impact on the young men who read this book! I am forever grateful for their support of this project!

Jermaine Zanders

Sean Bell

Jonathan McMillan

Dr. Ryan Ross

Renzo Minaya

TaMuk Scruggs

Dionizio Fisher

Matthew Davis

Dr. Craig McMullen

Otis Spears

Morris Jackson

Earl Garland

(Pictured in order: above L-R, then below L-R)

Dedication

I'd like to start off by acknowledging the behind the scenes support of my wife, Joy Sims. Thanks for doing all the things in our daily lives that allowed me to sit still for hours at a time working on this book. Without your support, I'd probably be still writing!

I'd also like to acknowledge Dr. Walter Milton, Lisa Petros, and the One-L Group Publishing family for their work on this project and for having a space for artists to get the most out of their work! Thanks, Lisa, for being a thought partner on aspects of the book. Thanks Dr. Milton for introducing me to Lisa and being an inspiration and mentor as well. It's greatly appreciated.

Finally, I'd like to thank all the young men I have encountered in my life to inspire me to write this book. Your hopes continue to push me to tell your stories, mentor and guide, and work on your behalf so you can make your futures look like your dreams.

BOYS ARE BRILLIANT!

ABOUT THE AUTHOR

DEDRICK J. SIMS

Dedrick J. Sims is the CEO & Founder of the Sims-Fayola Foundation. The Sims-Fayola Foundation focuses on improving the life outcomes of young men and boys of color by supporting schools and school districts, juvenile detention centers, parents, and other organizations focused on working with young men. The Sims-Fayola Foundation uses its three pillars of work as guideposts to improve their life outcomes. The three pillars are School Design and Support, Building Awareness, and Building Capacity.

Dedrick's career in urban education began in a high school classroom over 20 years ago as a substitute and he has since served in roles as a High School Biology and Chemistry Teacher, Secondary Curriculum Administrator, Master Lead Teacher, Technology Coordinator, Alternative School Teacher, Dean of Students, Assistant Principal and Principal of both traditional and charter public schools (Co-Ed and Single Gender), and school Founder.

Dedrick's commitment to education extends outside the classroom as well. As a published author of two other books as well as numerous professional articles, Dedrick uses his experience to build the capacity of others to serve students with informed excellence. As the CEO of the Sims-Fayola Foundation, Dedrick provides professional training to educators around the country in areas of single-gender learning, working with young men and boys of color, and school and program design through an equity lens. To date, through the Sims-Fayola Foundation, Dedrick's work has impacted over 10,000 young men and boys of color and provided workshops and coaching to over 2,000 professionals who work with young men and boys of color.

Dedrick recently was selected by Black Enterprise Magazine as one of the 100 Modern BE Men, has served his country as an officer in the United States Army, and is a proud member of Kappa Alpha Psi Fraternity, Inc.

Dedrick is an avid golfer and loves to read, travel, and do karaoke!

Table of Contents

TOPICS COVERED IN THIS BOOK

You Special Man 1

Can You Imagine? 4

Perspectives on Love 7

Money, Money, Money, Money……Money! 11

Pushing Through 13

Are You a Responsible Dude? 15

Grit…. Are You Gritty? 17

Death and Your Legacy 21

The Magnitude of Your Life 25

Uncertainty Once 27

What's Up With Peace? 31

What Is Faith? 33

Uncertainty Again 37

Let's Get Emotional 39

Let's Keep The Emotions Going 43

Your Image…. Don't Hurt Yourself 47

Let's Talk About Sex 51

Who Are Your Friends? 55

Yo Momma!…. That's Right I Said It 59

Winning…..Without Charlie Sheen Tiger Blood 61

Failure 66

You Special Man

Conversation 1

HEY MAN! I just want to take out some time to let you know how Special You Are. It is absolutely an honor to be a young man. You have the privilege of being the head of the household, the king, a leader in your community, and noticed by all as long as you walk in your maleness. As men, we are unique beings. We are usually looked to for leadership, wisdom, guidance, provision, and protection. Even the Bible talks about us being the primary sex in the chambers of the government. Your mother looks to you to be a male figure in the house even if your father is still there with you because men take care of the home, their mothers, and their siblings. So, I just wanted to take some time to encourage you today to walk in your maleness and be the best leader and young man you can be today. Take time to make the best decisions you can for yourself and the people around you. Your future is dependent on it. Now, have an unapologetically amazing day, and remember, We Just Talkin'! Now let's see what the fellas have to say about this.

- **From my man Earl Garland**

    Be the leader that you desire to follow. Observe the positive habits they have developed and find a way to incorporate them into your life. Always practice being the brilliant man you are. Even if there is no one to follow today, one day soon, you will be called on to lead in an area you never have before. If you stay ready, you don't have to get ready. I believe in you! You have something to offer the world that no one else could ever attempt. Don't wait for the right moment to find you; take this moment and make it right. Those around you will realize the possibility of their dreams by watching you live yours. The difference between those who dream and those that live out their dreams is ACTION. Take action and make your dreams your reality!

- **From my man Jermaine Zanders**

    Man, I know that people might say that you're only special if... and they finish that statement with all types of nouns and adjectives that ultimately limit who you are. Like, you're special if you can spit bars, or if you can throw and catch a ball you're special, or even that you're special based on your looks. I just want you to know that you're special because you are YOU! No one else on the face of this earth lives your life and can do what you do in the unique way you do it. So, live in your uniqueness, celebrate it, and don't ever let anyone limit or diminish who you are!

Can You Imagine?

Conversation 2

HEY MAN! Today I want to talk to you about the word Imagine. Imagine what you can do if you embrace who you really are as a young man. Imagine the impact you can have on your community when you step into your purpose. Imagine the stereotypes that will change when people realize how amazing and brilliant you really are. Can you imagine those things about yourself? Do you really believe that you are a king and a leader in your community and family? When you get up in the morning to get ready for school or work, do you feel like you have the power to change the world? To change someone's life? If you don't, let me inform you that you absolutely do! Imagining is important to me because it reminds me to imagine all that I can be if I don't put limits on myself. I know the news and the stereotypes floating around don't necessarily show us in the best light as a young man, but I know who I am, and I want you to know who you are. Do things today that will show people that they need to imagine you differently if they see you in a negative one now. You know who you are; they imagine who you are, but show them who you really are. So do your best again today in all you do, and imagine that you are already at the goals that you set for yourself and leading a beautiful and healthy family that's proud of you. Now, have an unapologetically amazing day, and remember, We Just Talkin'! Now let's see what the fellas have to say about this.

- **From my man Jermaine Zanders:**

    Do you know that your mind is one of the most powerful tools you have? That's because our minds allow us to imagine things and places that at times might seem far outside of our reach. I didn't think that I would have come as far as I have from where I started. My parents weren't rich, and my dad didn't even go to high school, yet I could not just go to college but ultimately earned two master's degrees. I imagined that I could make a difference in this world, and when I coupled that imagination with hope, paired that hope with faith, and followed all of them up with work, it went from being something I imagined to being my real life. I'm still imagining - this time that I will write books that will inspire people to live their best lives and make sure that NOTHING prevents that. What do you imagine? Are you dreaming bigger than what you see every day? If you're not, do me a favor and start dreaming right now because your dreams can live!

- **From my man Jonathan McMillan:**

    Imagine. Imagine big. Imagine often. Most people have trouble really imagining what they want because it doesn't feel natural to them. They've been told to be realistic all of their lives, so they tend to dream small. They doubt what they can achieve with even a little bit of direction and focus. The life they would love to live in their ultimate fantasies is "too good to come true." And while getting anything your heart desires is much more complicated than simply wishing upon a star, you create the life you dream of by first identifying what that dream consists of and then devising a plan to build it. An essential step in creating and living the life you want to live is seeing it and stating it in the present tense. The more detailed the picture in your mind of what your goal looks like once achieved, the greater the energy and effort you will exert to make it a reality faster. Close your eyes and picture what life looks like after achieving your goal. Where are you? Who's around you? What do you do every day as a result of achieving your goal? It is equally important to imagine how it will feel when you achieve your goal. What if you...

> ...focused the power of imagination on how good it would feel to achieve something good and future and successes? How much more would you accomplish if you emotionalized pride? How much bigger and significant would the goals you set be? Chances are they would be better than average. Just be careful to not use the powers of imagine against yourself. Fear is imagination gone bad. It is an emotion that motivates people to create and achieve goals so insignificant they are practically subconscious. Imagining what it feels like to fail keeps most people from ever trying anything new, taking any risks, or trying their best and going the extra mile. However, doing those very things is precisely what will help you build the life of your dreams. So again, young man, imagine. Imagine big. Imagine often.

- **From my man Dionizio Fisher**
  > I agree. As men, especially men of color, we grow up faced with seeing images of ourselves in the news, television, music videos, social media, and the big screen showing us as angry, violent, uncaring, and unproductive. People think we are only concerned with fast cars, pretty women and lots of money. Because of this, many of us who spend, or have spent, any considerable amount of time watching and/or being fed these images from all these sources (myself included) tend to limit our imagination and ideas about ourselves and who we can be. It was hard for me to imagine, or believe, that I could do anything, or be anything, other than being a low producing, low earning, drain on society when I was growing up. It wasn't until I became an adult and began surrounding myself with positive people and actively changing the images and voices that I allowed into my mind. I finally started to see all possibilities of a positive life of fulfillment and achievement within my grasp. I learned that half of you are, is who you think you are. If you believe that you are unimportant or "bad," that's almost surely exactly what you'll become. But if you believe in yourself or allow your imagination to run free, you can build any future you want to create for yourself.

Perspectives on Love

Conversation 3

HEY MAN! Today I want to talk to you about love. I'm not talking about the love between a boy and a girl; I'm talking about loving yourself. I'm talking about loving yourself enough to love the fact that you are unique. Yes, you, as a boy, are unique! The chromosomes had to line up perfectly to produce you! So, today, make it a point to show YOU some love! Find things throughout the day that reflect the way you love yourself. I know this conversation about love can sometimes be skewed and imaged as soft. But, there is nothing weak about showing love, especially to yourself. The way you carry yourself in school and life reflects how you feel about yourself. I read this thing one time before that said how you treat others reflects how you feel about yourself. So, how are you treating people today? Are you showing others love because you love yourself? Are you giving others the benefit of the doubt today because you give yourself the benefit of the doubt? Today could be a great day because you can make it one with love. Anyway, love yourself and love others. Remember, the world is counting on you to be a leader of love and show love to all. Now, have an unapologetically amazing day, and remember, We Just Talkin'! Now let's see what the fellas have to say about this.

- **From my man Otis Spears:**

    Learning to love and appreciate yourself will be an essential lesson in life. As a teen, I always sought approval from people who really didn't respect me, let alone loved me. It took a lot of disappointment to wake up and start approving myself by FIRST, loving myself! Loving yourself will always protect you from all the voices that will tell you that you're not worth anything and no one loves you. As long as you remember how valuable you are to this world and you are unique in the eyes of the Almighty, nothing can stop you! It's impossible to love others if you never took the time to learn how to love yourself. So start today and write down what makes you special? What makes you unique? You will discover whatever you write about yourself will be a reason to love yourself. Loving yourself will build confidence, strength, and a positive attitude. Loving yourself will reveal that it's not hard to love others. Everyone needs love, and the best way to show that love is to RESPECT one another. So hopefully, this will trigger your heart to start loving your fellow man and never think less of yourself! I share this with you in love, and whenever you feel down, read this and remember...Love conquers all!

- **From my man Jonathan McMillan:**

    Let's talk about love. A word that is often overused and misused. People say they love things that they really just like and tell others that they love them to get what they want from those people. To me, love is the feeling you have for something or someone you need in your life, like water and air and nourishment. Or to love someone is to be incapable of intentionally hurting that person, whether physically or emotionally. It's never a tool or weapon. Instead, it should serve as inspiration that drives you to be your best for that which and whom you love, most of all yourself. You can show yourself love, by the standards and the goals you set for yourself. Never settle for less than what you deserve from yourself or others. Love demands this much. Love also requires you to respect yourself and your environment. Again, suppose you love someone, including yourself, your body, the planet you live on, and the human race. In that case, you are incapable of intentionally hurting any of those physically, spiritually, or emotionally. So, as we're talking, remember to speak to yourself with love because you are worthy of love and loveable, especially from yourself.

BOYS ARE YEARNING FOR SUCCESS

Money, Money, Money, Money......Money!

Conversation 4

HEY MAN! Another day, another dollar! Yep, today's topic is about Money, Money, Money.....MONEY! Remember that song? If not, google it! Money was my focus when I was younger. I grew up poor, and it seemed like only money could solve our problems. I felt like my life and friends would be better if we had enough money! Now, it's more like another day, another accomplishment; or another day, another opportunity to make a difference in someone else's life. Man, how my life and the way I think have changed. I'm inviting you to start thinking like that as well today. As I mentioned in an earlier conversation, we are looked upon as the guiders of our communities as a man. Not that women don't play a role because they do, but as I stated before, the world looks to a man to be the leader in many situations. So, the question is, how are you going to show leadership today that has nothing to do with the money? How are you going to help someone else today without making it rain? I have a suggestion! How about looking for another young man to mentor who is younger than you or looks up to you to help. Improve yourself by helping him improve himself. Does this make sense? Remember this rule that I think of often, "As we teach, we learn." This means we have to be on point before telling somebody else how to be on point. Now, have an unapologetically amazing day, and remember, We Just Talkin'! Now let's see what the fellas have to say about this.

- **From my man Morris Jackson:**

    Money, though needed to meet specific standards of living, shouldn't drive us. Accomplishing goals should. Assisting and improving the lives of others should motivate us. And improving our current situations should inspire us. There's always room for improvement. If Lebron James (The most physically gifted basketball player on earth) says he has room to grow, we ALL have room to grow in our endeavors. THAT should motivate us!

- **From my man in Los Angeles:**

    Hey young man, I've got a question for you - Is money necessary? Absolutely it is, as it provides us with the opportunity to provide for our families, take care of our daily needs, and allow us to secure some (if not all) our wants. However, many men (young and old) have lost the ability to provide for their families and take care of their needs and wants because they fell in love with money. The Bible states, "for the love of money is the root of all evil." This simply means that typically, nothing good comes about when we FOCUS more on money than other important things like faith, family, and friendships. If you focus on these three things early on in life, your outlook on money's place in your life will become very clear.

Pushing Through

Conversation 5

HEY MAN! There will be days when you just don't feel like being the man you know you are. They can start off well, but something can trigger us and just throw the rest of the day off. Your mood changes, and the day can be challenging in general. That's why today's conversation about Pushing Through! Say it with your chest, man! PUSHING THROUGH! On days like this, you may find yourself treating people horribly, disrespectfully, or not as good as you are supposed to and potentially harming a relationship that you value. So, the question is, what do you do during the hard days? Do you hide and not go out into the world? Do you just let people have it because you're having a bad day, or do you dig deep and work against the negative feelings and emotions that you're having? I hope you dig deep and recapture the man you know you are. Emotions are temporary, and they sometimes make you think something is happening when it's actually not. They can make you believe that someone is looking at you when they are actually not. They can make you think someone is talking about you when they actually are not. They can also make you believe that a situation is far worse than it actually is when it's not. So, if today is one of those days for you, I challenge you to dig deep and be the man you know you are for yourself and those around you who may be looking to you. Now, have an unapologetically amazing day, and remember, We Just Talkin'! Now let's see what the fellas have to say about this.

- **From my man in Los Angeles:**

  We've all had them "those days." As I'm sitting here typing this, I can recall several of "those days" over the past year. I can honestly say that I have not always taken my own advice on what I'm about to suggest; however, now is a good time for the both of us to incorporate what's next. Try not to take things that happen to you personally, as you can only control what you can control. I tend to believe that most people are good and intend to do what's right. So, when someone does something that is clearly not right, the natural tendency should be to try not to take it personally. If you can take the time to put yourself in that person's shoes, you may better understand what drove the person's actions. In most instances, if your response to the situation is positive, the situation will also turn out positive. Give it a try, and I think you will start to see fewer of "those days."

- **From my man TaMuk Scruggs**

  Having contemplated and attempted suicide, I've had some tough days. Sometimes, I would mentally retreat to my dark place, which caused me to do destructive things. Other days, when I had people in my life that truly loved me, I would talk with them about life, music, basketball, and love. These sessions helped get my mind healthy. Once I got better mentally, I used basketball to get better physically. It ended the depression. There will be days when life will beat you up, but if you surround yourself with people that love you, you will survive the hard days to experience the good days and love. So, find out what helps you feel good, and remember, we're just talkin'!

Are You a Responsible Dude?

Conversation 6

HEY MAN, I want to talk to you today about Responsibility. The word, responsibility can be a very intimidating word for some people. It indicates that you are being held accountable for something or someone other than yourself or your stuff. Some days it's hard to be held responsible for ourselves, let alone someone or something else! So being held accountable for somebody else's action or inaction can be very intimidating and seem downright unfair. But as I said before, the truth is that as a young man, the world looks to us to be responsible. The world looks to us to be responsible for ourselves, our communities, and our families. So, I'm asking you today to be responsible for your life outcome. What I mean is that I want you to be responsible for where you end up in life. So, go out today and set a goal for yourself, dream big, and take responsibility for making it happen for you, your family, and those who you would impact that you haven't even met yet. Now, have an unapologetically amazing day, and remember, We Just Talkin'! Now let's see what the fellas have to say about this.

- **From my man in Los Angeles:**

    Ironically, this section is an excellent follow-up to my last few words for you when I suggested that a positive response to situations can drive positive results. Of course, the word Responsibility carries a lot of weight, and it can be intimidating, but why make it more difficult than it has to be?? What do I mean - watch this: If you'll notice, the root word in Responsibility is Response. So, in essence, if you can always seek to find that positive Response to life situations, no matter how difficult, you are well on your way to being the Responsible young man you were destined to be. Remember, your Response can and will drive your level of Responsibility.

- **From my man TaMuk Scruggs:**

    It's a big word. It's an even bigger weight to carry. Most run from it like it is their broke cousin at the family reunion that everyone knows is going to either ask you for money or just plain rob you. The thing is, and listen, we're just talkin', you can run from it, but you can't hide from it. As an adult, as a MAN, you will always have responsibilities, whether they be to your family, yourself, or your community. I learned that my daughters were my responsibilities, and loving and providing guidance to them was what I was supposed to do even though I had no clue how; nevertheless, it had to be done. Life is like that; even if we don't want to do what is right, it still has to be done, so keep your head up and keep moving forward!

Grit.... Are You Gritty?

Conversation 7

HEY MAN, I want to talk to you today about a word called Grit. You show grit whenever you push past something challenging and make it happen anyway. Grit is what your parents display when they pay all the bills, make sure you eat, and buy other things even though they don't have all the money. Grit is what you show when you are studying for a test late at night, and you're tired, but you continue to push through anyway because you know you have to do it. In other words, Grit is having HEART! Grit is an excellent characteristic to have. You often face an obstacle but do not necessarily have all the tools needed to accomplish that goal with ease. That's when you have to exhibit grit. So today, I want you to think about the word grit when you come across a hard part of your day today. You may have to exhibit Grit and discipline to not get into an argument with someone today. You may have to display grit when you go home and have to deal with your parents or your siblings. Just remember that having grit is a good thing. Now, have an unapologetically amazing day, and remember, We Just Talkin'! Now let's see what the fellas have to say about this.

- **From my man in Los Angeles:**

    When I think about the word Grit, I'm reminded of a great American city where I had the opportunity to live for nearly seven years. If you follow the NBA, you may know that the Memphis Grizzlies professional basketball team is also known as the team of Grit and Grind. This label has a lot to do with the Team's belief in doing the basic dirty work (rebounding, diving for loose balls, setting hard screens, etc.) required to compete with some of the other big market teams in its conference. Memphis, TN, is the perfect city for a Gritty team, as this great American city has had to endure its share of Grit and resilience to overcome some dark days in this Nation's history. During the height of the Civil Rights movement on April 4, 1968, Memphis, TN, became the overwhelming center of attention when Dr. Martin Luther King, Jr. was assassinated there. In my opinion, few American cities could have overcome such a dark time in World history; however, the people of Memphis, TN, used their Grit to embrace the events by honoring Dr. King's legacy and is now one of the most visited cities in the US today. Like Memphis, TN, you too can and should your Grit to overcome the darkest days and circumstances in your life. Perhaps, your exhibition of Grit will provide the motivation for someone else to press on and overcome the most troubling times in their lives.

- **From my man Dr. Craig McMullen**

    I grew up with a living example of GRIT. My father lost his dad when he was only 10 years old and took on the responsibility of helping his mother raise his younger siblings among the rural poverty of the Great Depression. By the age of 14, he left home to make a living on his own – that took some GRIT! GRIT is also the measurement for different types of sandpaper that rate from "coarse to fine." The different levels of grit on the sandpaper are used to sand down a rough object until it becomes smooth. GRIT is what a person finds inside themselves when they hit a rough patch. Grit takes the difficult hand that life deals you and refuses to fold, but instead calls the "bluff" and pushes all the chips in, believing that you have in your hand all you need to be successful. That was the bet my father demonstrated with his grit when he struck out on his own as a young teenager in the face of an unknown future. GRIT is the sandpaper of negative challenges that refines the greatness inside of you! Don't quit! Instead, use the problems in front of you to knock off the rough edges of your life and look at the best you emerging.

Death and Your Legacy

Conversation 8

HEY MAN! Today I want to talk to you about Death & Legacy! Last night was a very rough night for me. I tossed and turned and hardly got any sleep because I was dreaming about death. Yes, death! I know it's not a subject many people want to talk about, but it's an inevitable part of living. One day we will all leave this earth and go to another place. It had me reflecting on my place in this world and what kind of legacy I wanted to leave behind. It forced me to think about who I am as a man and who I want to be remembered. I'm not asking you to start thinking about death, but I am asking you to start thinking about what kind of legacy you would like to leave as a man in this world. Will it be a legacy of violence, bad decisions, irresponsibility, and running away from problems? Will it be a legacy of responsibility, being a great friend and father, having done your best in school and life, and leaving a legacy of helping people? I want you to think about that today and view every action you take and every conversation you have today from that lens. Ask yourself, did what I just do add or subtract to the legacy that I want to leave? Did what I just say add or subtract to the legacy that I want to leave? Thinking about life in this way is sort of like making a will. Most people do not think about wills because they don't want to think about death or think it's too far away to really be relevant right now. The truth is we must all think about the final moments of our lives and what we would want people to remember us by. I know this is a serious conversation, but it's really needed. Now, have an unapologetically amazing day, and remember, We Just Talkin'! Now let's see what the fellas have to say about this.

- **From my man Otis Spears:**

    As men, we are here to serve the world with our unique abilities. You have something within that is meant to come out that will speak of the legacy you will leave behind one day. From Abraham Lincoln to Malcolm X, many greats have left a legacy that will be remembered until the end of time. Statues and buildings are dedicated to those who contributed their genius and ideas in making mankind a better experience to live. What is it that you have a burning passion to display that will one day make you a legend? There are enough people who rather live an average life. Make sure that you're not one of them! You're meant to leave a legacy for your family, your community, and the world. Always strive to reach the top of the cliff because the bottom of the mountain, it's filled with many who are afraid to build a legacy. Every day, someone is reporting or writing about the legacy of a brilliant person; why not you? Begin to decide that your life will be remembered in a Library and not in a one-page obituary. Greatness is calling you, pay attention to it and start the journey in creating your legacy NOW!

- **From my man in Los Angeles:**

    Hey young man - I've got another question for you. How long do you think it takes to build a Legacy: one year, five years, 25 years, or a lifetime?? Honestly, any of the time as mentioned above frames could be correct. However, I genuinely believe a Legacy can be built instantaneously by a single action or a one-time personal encounter. Given that we live in a "perception is reality" society, unfortunately, we are sometimes not allowed to make a second impression. And, whereas it may take some time to build a Legacy, one ill-advised action can immediately damage that same Legacy. So, my challenge to you is to treat every action and encounter as if your life's Legacy depended on it - START YOUR LEGACY NOW!!

The Magnitude of Your Life

Conversation 9

HEY MAN! I woke up today thinking about my life and how I am living it. Am I on the right track? Am I doing what I am supposed to be doing? How do people see me? I'm sure you have done the same at some point. If not, I encourage you to ask yourself these questions. Today is about the Magnitude of Your Life! Life is not just about waking up every day, going to school, coming home or hanging out with your friends, eating dinner, and going to sleep. Each day we live, we impact others and nature around us. We leave a footprint somewhere every day. Whether in school, at home, at the bus stop, in the mall, at the movies, or just walking down the street. We leave a mark. So, taking time to reflect on the impact of your mark is beneficial to you and those you have impacted and those you will impact. As a young man, it's important to assess the magnitude of your maleness on things and the people around you. I encourage you to take some time today and think about these things. Now, have an unapologetically amazing day, and remember, We Just Talkin'! Now let's see what the fellas have to say about this.

- **From my man Jermaine Zanders:**

    HEY MAN, I was thinking about this idea of impacting others. When I was your age, I didn't know people even paid attention to my presence. That feeling continued into adulthood, even once I began my teaching career. What I realized, though, was that even if they never say anything directly to you, people are watching what you do; they're watching how you handle stress; they're observing your reactions when things don't go your way. While some people may be silently judging you, others are watching you as a model. They see your natural swagger, and they want to be able to deal with things the way you deal with them. So, please know that you're setting an example, even when you don't think you are. Keep on doing you, and watch how many folks want to follow your lead!

- **From my man TaMuk Scruggs**

    There are days when you will come in contact with people, and your life will be changed. The reason is that they are here to leave an IMPACT on your life. But, there will also be days when YOU will be the person that will alter the course of someone's life. See, we're all bound by cosmic strings. Some are beautiful tight little bows, and others, well, others are fragile, ragged, knotted up balls of barbed wire. The thing is, living your life's purpose will determine if your string will be a beautiful bow tied to their string. Should you not be living your purpose, it could just be the string that cuts them and your relationship to shreds. So, decide every day whether or not you'd like to be the gift with the bow on top of the barbed wire, slicing people up damaging them for someone else.

Uncertainty Once

Conversation 10

HEY MAN, this life is crazy! Today is about Uncertainty! Basically, it's when you just don't know. I bet you've said that to yourself many times. Sometimes we just don't understand some of the things that happen around or to us. One day we feel very confident and on top of the world, and the next day, we feel like we don't know what the heck is going on. So what do we do in times like these when we seem to lose our focus and question what we thought was important to us? I don't know that I have an answer that's the "final answer," but I know that the answer was to keep pushing in my life. Keep moving by all means! Do your best not to wallow in this uncertainty. Keep moving forward even if you don't know what you are moving forward to. I know that sounds weird, but it's wise. Because one day, you will not feel so uncertain anymore, and you don't want to have just been sitting still and not making any progress towards anything. Does this make sense?

I'll use the example of a car race. If you are racing in the Indianapolis 500, one of the premier NASCAR racing events, all cars go roaring off but you when the light turns green. You are sitting in your car paralyzed by uncertainty, so you don't hit the gas pedal. You are not sure if you want to be in the race or not, so you do nothing. Then, about two minutes later, you decide that racing is ok with you again, and you decide to hit the gas. However, because you have sat still and did not take off with the others, you are really behind and have so much ground to make up for. Had you at least kept moving and taken off with the others, you would not have been so far behind and would have had a better chance at still winning the race. That's what I mean when I say to keep pushing. So, if today is one of those days or weeks where you don't understand what's happening around you and feel uncertain about what you used to feel sure about, just keep pushing. Have an unapologetically amazing day, and remember, We Just Talkin'! Now let's see what the fellas have to say about this.

- **From my man Jermaine Zanders:**

    Man! I can't tell you how many times I've wondered how I made it through some of the roughest times of my life. How did this dude from Uptown New Orleans, get through a house fire, Hurricane Katrina, Hurricane Isaac, and so many personal trials over the years? The answer is really simple – one step at a time, one moment at a time. I wish I could tell you there was some magic answer to how we persevere even when we don't think we can, but honestly, there really isn't a magic remedy. I do believe, however, that persevering in the face of what seems like insurmountable odds is just written into the fabric of our DNA. I remember during Hurricane Isaac that devastated areas outside of New Orleans, LA in 2012, my brother, sister-in-law, their 6-month-old son, and our teenage nephew waded through waist-deep, sometimes chest-deep water. That was one of the scariest times in my life. When we stepped outside their flooded house, saw our flooded automobiles, it hit me – we don't have the option of giving up. We had to step out into the water-filled streets where anything could have been swimming in the water, and we had to make it to safety. How did we get there, one...

> ...careful step at a time!   At times we had to run, and at times we had to take a break, but mostly just one step at a time. We eventually made it to safety. So, when you're flooded with emotions and the tumultuous waters of life seem like they're going to overtake you, I encourage you to keep taking one step at a time, run forward if you have to; take a short break if you have to, but by all means keep moving, because eventually, you'll make it higher ground!

- **From my man TaMuk Scruggs**
  > There are some days when I just don't know for sure what the hell the Universe is expecting from me. So I roll out of bed, hit the crapper, and have too seriously contemplate the meaning of life and my place in it. By the time I am done, though, someone has asked me a question that only I can answer for them, which reminds me of my purpose. It reminds me that even though I may not always want to, I gotta crap or get off the pot because life doesn't stop even when you don't want to go on. And to quit on yourself is to deny others of being where they're supposed to be for their possible blessings. So always keep tissue because you can only sit on the throne for so long until your feet go to sleep.

What's Up With Peace?

Conversation 11

HEY MAN, how do you define Peace? When you think of Peace, what comes to your mind? It's not easy for me to explain Peace because I feel like it has escaped me. Yes, even now, Peace is elusive to me. There are times where I feel like I am at Peace, but then life happens, and it fades as fast as it appeared. A fleeting feeling of peace is to me. If I tried to define Peace now, it would be being ok with where I am in my life walk. Are you alright with where you are in your life walk? Are you at Peace with the man that you are or developing into? When you get up in the morning, are you ok with who you see in the mirror looking back at you? We need to ask and answer these questions if we are going to impact the world that we want to as men. I think you can only make a true impact on others if you are at Peace with who you are. That Peace gives you the courage to just act as you feel. Does that make sense? With Peace in your heart, you are ok with what you are doing and why you are doing it. I'm continuing to grow in my search for my own true Peace, and I encourage you to do the same. I want to be the best man you can be for others and myself, and I have a good idea that Peace is a key factor in that happening. Have an unapologetically amazing day, and remember, We Just Talkin'! Now let's see what the fellas have to say about this.

- **From my man Sean Bell**

    Within my forty-something years, I have determined a few things about Peace. Peace is something that you must fight for. There are so many distractions in this world that try and take it away from us. Usually, when we think of distractions, we think of outside threats that we cannot necessarily control. However, we are our own determiners of our Peace, and many times it is our own emotions, doubts, and fears that disturb it. We can be in the middle of a peaceful beach, with the calm of the waves and the refreshing wind, and not have Peace of mind. We talk about what makes a man a man, but having Peace is not taught, and acting like things don't bother us is not the same thing as having Peace. As men, we try to give the illusion that we are strong and unbothered, but the truth is that many of us are not fighting for Peace, and the very things that we try to protect are at risk because of it. I really wished that someone took the time to share this with me growing up. I was told not to cry, to say it with your chest, to brush myself off, and to never quit. I wasn't told that I would need peace to get through my struggles, achieve in life, or be the hardest thing to maintain. Without it, we can obtain the American dream but not be able to truly enjoy it. Without Peace, we cannot truly live the lives we were put on this earth to live. Without Peace, we cannot only lose our minds but our lives. Remember these words FIGHT FOR PEACE! Not In a demonstration or for the world but the world inside of you. This may look different depending on what gives you Peace, but most of us know what Peace is to us, so do what you need to do to obtain it and FIGHT to keep it. You can speak it, listen to a song, take a trip, have positive self-talk, and spend time in meditation and prayer. But by all means, share with someone else (that you trust) when you are not at Peace with yourself. At my job, we have a mantra that we tell our students, "Don't suffer in silence!" FIGHT FOR PEACE!

What Is Faith?

Conversation 12

HEY MAN! Today I want to talk to you about Faith. No, this will not be a conversation about religion or anything like that. Faith operates in many aspects outside of the context of religion. To have faith is to strongly believe that something will happen without it having happened yet. Does this make sense? Faith operates in many aspects outside of the context of religion. To have faith is to strongly believe that something will happen without it having happened yet. Does this make sense? For example, if you tell your parents that you need a new pair of shoes for an event that is very important to you, you may have faith that they will take care of your needs. Now, as it relates to religion, faith is to believe in the promises of God as they are written in the Bible, even if you don't see them right now. That's probably the faith that you are most accustomed to hearing about. As a man, it is important to have faith that things will turn out the way they are supposed to for you to walk in your authentic self. Likewise, your family and children will have to have faith that you would do the right thing for them regardless of any outside pressure to do things differently. I have to admit; faith is a challenging concept. It's hard to believe in things that you don't see. However, in my experience, when I have faith in something, and it actually happens, it strengthens my faith even more and makes me excited about things that are to come that may not be a reality right now. So, today I want you to think about what you have faith for and practice strengthening your faith for the things that will meet you in the future and help you become the best man you could be. Have an unapologetically amazing day, and remember We Just Talkin'! Now let's see what the fellas have to say about this.

- **From my man Dr. Craig McMullen**

    The Bible defines "faith" as having confidence in what we hope for and assurance about what we do not see. (Chapter 11 and Verse 1 in the book of Hebrews). Back in the 1980's urban America was facing a new epidemic on its streets. The invention of crack cocaine spread out among innocent young lives killing thousands by use or the violence that accompanied it. Many communities came under the siege of gangs battling over the control of the sale of this drug. Several clergy and activists from Roxbury started "Drop-A-Dime-Report-Crime," a community crime watch group. But to empower others to join this movement, we decided to hold all-night prayer vigils in local crack houses. We put our faith in our hope for a drug-free neighborhood by our actions. We faced the gangs with our confident faith in what we could not see in the present violent streets but instead had hope for what our neighborhood could become. Today, as you begin your day, don't get paralyzed by the epidemics in front of you; instead, choose to have faith that you have in your hope the antidote that will cure your life and community.

- **From my man Sean Bell**

    Faith is one of the hardest things to speak of because either you have it or you don't. When you do have it, it's blind, so you never know how much of it you truly have until it's tested. Sometimes faith is a belief in something without true evidence that it will come to pass. And once that evidence is seen, our faith starts to build and gets bigger and bigger until we are certain about that thing we once were so uncertain of. We put our faith in things all the time. Our cars, to get us from point A to point B, the buildings that we live and visit from day to day. However, it's very hard to put our faith in ourselves or something bigger than ourselves, like a movement of God. I think this is because we can see the evidence of our decisions, accomplishments, and mistakes. It takes real vulnerability to put our trust in something bigger than us or our situation. Learn sooner or later to put your faith in that inner voice that leads you, the abilities and gifts that you were given, and never lose faith in people. Faith will help you achieve what you want and be accountable for your role in the bigger picture. Faith will lead you to your destiny.

Uncertainty Again

Conversation 13

HEY MAN! Today I want to talk to you AGAIN about Uncertainty! Uncertainty does not know the next step. It could be the next step in your life, career, relationship, etc. It's just the fact that you don't know. Uncertainty can be downright scary. As men, our nature is to be in control, and having uncertainty definitely rocks that boat. When I feel uncertain, I feel insecure to a degree. I feel unsure of myself, and that's not a good feeling for me. I'm sure it's not for you either. I'm the kind of cat that needs to know what's next. You probably are too. When was the last time you felt uncertain? What was it about? What ended up happening? Did you talk to anyone about it? However, I have learned that even in uncertainty, you have to keep moving forward. To not do anything because of uncertainty is not good for you. So, the next time you feel uncertain about the next step………keep stepping! Have an unapologetically amazing day, and remember, We Just Talkin'!

- **From my man Renzo Minaya**

    My man! How do I even begin to tell you that it was the times in my life when I felt uncertain about my future that I realized it was just a challenge for me to dream bigger! You see, uncertainty is part of every single person's life. Without uncertainty, there is no sense of purpose or motivation to do something great. I remember being in my senior year in high school and having absolutely no idea what I wanted to do after I graduated. Man, I was so lost that I just didn't even know what to answer people when they asked me about my aspirations, goals, dreams, career choice, you name it! Those were some tough times. I was so uncertain about my future that I felt out of place like I just didn't belong where I was. After high school, I had so many jobs just because I was looking for someplace to belong, a purpose for living my life. But then there was a breakthrough; it was at one of my first jobs at a Movie Theater. The manager said that he saw a lot of potential in me and wanted me to become a supervisor. Me? are you sure? I said. I mean, how could he see potential in someone who was so unsure of life. Well, he just saw me being me, utilizing my talents, and being able to help others. That's it. Many years have gone by since that movie theater manager gave me that big break. Today I can live my life with a sense of purpose because to keep moving forward, doing the right thing, being myself, and utilizing my talents to help others. I genuinely believe that if you find out what your talents are and choose to use them to help other people, you will have a lot more certainty in your life, and you will make a difference in this world. So, remember, without uncertainty, there is no sense of purpose or motivation to do something great, so go out and do it, champ!

Let's Get Emotional

Conversation 14

HEY MAN! Today is not such a good day for me, so I thought it would be good to talk to you about Emotions! I'm reeling from a hit to my soul from some pretty tough emotions. It's the kind of emotions that leave you debilitated and deflated and unable to engage in life. I'm faced with a choice to succumb to these emotions and stay in this place of pain or try to push through and live. This is a time where I should try to access a friend, but I just don't want to talk to anyone. That's why I'm writing to you. What do you do when you feel this way? Do you ever feel this way? Some think that we should not feel this way as men; that men should be harder than this. I say that's crap! We have feelings too, and it's not soft to show them. In fact, it's quite brave and courageous to show them. What do you do now when you feel hurt, angry, sad, or miserable? People respond in different ways to these kinds of emotions, but we must be really aware as men and leaders how we process these emotions because they can severely impact our leadership and decisions. Because we know we are leaders of our families and communities, negatively impacting our emotions is quite serious. I don't always get this one right, so I am excited to see what the fellas have to say about this one. Have an unapologetically amazing day, and remember, man, We Just Talkin'! Now, let's see what the fellas have to say about this.

- **From my man Matthew Davis**

    HEY MAN, Let's Get Emotional. "What? Emotions?! Next, you're gonna tell me about feelings, and I don't know about those. My dad always told me to be tough and not let others see me as weak. He said my mom needed me to be strong because she was going through a tough time, which seems like it has lasted most of my life. Plus, my older brother seems to have enough emotions for both of us. He's always getting himself into problems because he overreacts. So, I have to do what I can to make things easier for everyone else at home. Like the time my mom and dad got into a fight after my dad lost his job. I could tell my dad was trying to stay strong, but my mom was yelling a lot, and my dad finally let his emotions go--and it wasn't pretty. I've only seen him get that mad a couple times. But he can get loud and mean when he does. He called my mom a lot of names that made her cry even worse. Then my brother got involved, and that didn't help anything. I wish he would just shut up and leave it alone. But I wasn't about to tell him that and make things even worse. So, I just hugged my mom and stayed strong, though I might've let a teardrop or two fall out of the swelling water in my eye. I couldn't help it that night. Staying strong helped me in school sometimes too. When other kids...

...tried to mess with me, I never let them see that it got to me, even if it hurt a little. But they stopped messing, so I guess I did alright. My dad was different after that fight with my mom. He actually told me that it's good to let my feelings out sometimes so I don't blow up later. So, I've been trying to let people know when I get mad, sad, or scared. Scared is a hard one though, it still doesn't feel right to talk about it, even with my mom. Sometimes I can feel all the feelings I have stacked up inside, and it feels like I'm about to blow. But I usually take a deep breath and feel my jaw get real tight. I still gotta learn how to let it all out, but I think my dad was right--I can't keep these emotions locked up forever. They're gonna come out one way or another, so I might as well do it how I want, instead of letting others push me to it. I'm glad I have my mom and dad around for that and my best friend. So, let's get emotional, man...take control of those feelings now before they control you later.

Let's Keep The Emotions Going

Conversation 15

HEY MAN! Today I want to talk to you more about Emotions. Emotions are a powerful thing in your life. They can either help you or hurt you. They are very deceptive though. Sometimes I can make you feel like something is happening when it's really not. You may take action against something because you feel like it's against you when it's really not. Emotions landed a lot of people in jail and in the grave. They can help you as well, though. Positive emotions can cause you to take action and do something very good for yourself or for someone else. Positive emotions make you feel good about yourself as well. As a young man, people sometimes associate negative emotions with us, but we sometimes suppress them because we are taught that they are not manly. However, for us to be effective in life, we must learn to manage our emotions. We must turn tonight live by our emotions alone. Remember I told you that they could be deceptive sometimes. I remember my emotions told me that my girlfriend was cheating on me, and I accused her of that and became very upset. I said some things that I would read, which hurt her feelings. Not only did it hurt her feelings, but also it hurt our relationship. In the end, when I found out that what I was feeling was not true, I had to apologize, but I also lost a lot of respect from her. That was when my emotions were negative and led me to do something that I regret. Does that make sense to you? So today, I want you to pay attention to your emotions and what they tempt you to do. Try to control your emotions so they won't lead you down the wrong path. Try hard to replace negative emotions with positive ones. Try even harder to project positive emotions as interact with people today. Have an unapologetically amazing day, and remember, man, We Just Talkin'! Now, let's see what the fellas have to say about this.

- **From my man Renzo Minaya**

    Man! I still remember the first time I really expressed hatred towards someone. I was 9 years old, and my parents had separated, we had moved to the U.S., and I had no idea what was happening. I just didn't know how to feel except angry. Angry because I never understood why he left us, why he abandoned us, why he chose not to come here with us. Al I knew was that I was expected to be the man of the house, whatever that meant! I was just a kid. Since I was expected to be "the man of the house," I was also told that I needed to act like a man and that crying was for girls; therefore, I was not allowed to express how sad I felt or anything like that. But as I got older, I learned that feelings were not a bad thing and that feeling happy, sad, angry, or afraid was normal. There really isn't...

...anything wrong with feeling a certain way, but what you do with those feelings and how you react based on how you feel is what really matters. Well, I chose not to allow the hatred that I had towards my father to control me. It wasn't until I was 24 years old that I realized just how much I hated my father and how much I had pushed older men away from me because of being abandoned by my father. Not having the freedom to express my feelings to someone else hurt people I loved and kept them from loving me. I finally got a chance to reconnect with my father at the age of 27, and I took the time to let him know I forgave him. I came to find out that my father never had a good relationship with his father and that he was taught not to express his feelings, and he didn't know how to express love towards me. In other words, you never know what other people are going through and how hard it is for them to express how they feel. But if we all take a moment to think about how others feel and why they feel that way, we will realize that we are all trying to manage our emotions one way or another. The goal is to now allow your emotions to dictate your actions. If we can do that, we will be in a much better place, one day at a time. I believe you can do it, champ!

Your Image....
Don't Hurt Yourself

Conversation 16

HEY MAN! Today I want to talk to you about your Image! Do you take pride in your appearance? Not just your clothes. I'm talking about your whole look, your hair, teeth, nails, and eyes. Yes, I'm talking about it all. The way you look is important because it's the first thing people see when they meet you. They don't know how much you know or how well you speak yet, but they know what they see. If they see something that turns them off, you might not ever get to show them who you really are...and that's dangerous as a young man because this can negatively impact your ability to lead. So, what do people see when they look at you? Are you dressed sharply and kept neatly all the time? Don't get me wrong, I'm not saying you have to be suited and booted every day with the latest fashion gear. In fact, you can have on some old clothes and still positively impact how someone sees you because it's not what you have on, it's how you wear it. I've known people who have worn the same clothes multiple times during a week, but it was always clean and very presentable. They understood the power of the first impression, and so should you. How do you look today? Has anyone made a comment on how you look today? If so, and it was a negative comment, do you know why it was negative? Think about it the same if it was a positive comment. Look, in the end, the way you present yourself is super important to your future. So, I am asking you to make a conscious attempt each day to present yourself the best way you can, both with your physical appearance, what you say, and how you think. Have an unapologetically amazing day, and remember, man, We Just Talkin'! Now let's see what the fellas have to say about this.

- **From my man Dr. Ryan Ross:**

    Say, little brother...I'm glad we are just talking. I'm not preaching, teaching, and just talking and hoping that I have something that works listening to. I remember when I was 11 years old, eleven was a rough year. That year my mom couldn't get any seasonal work, and we got cut off food stamps, so money was not an option and food felt like a dream. I decided I would go hustle because I have never been afraid of a hard day's work. I went to the local liquor store because of an African American gentleman, only I figured if I asked him to take out his trash or maybe sweep the sidewalk, he would pay me some money. I could buy some ramen noodles and ground beef some my brothers and sisters could eat. I learned a lesson that day, but I have never forgotten, " Sir, my name is Ryan, and I wanted to see if I could take out your trash or sweep the sidewalk for $5 trying to make some money so my brothers and sisters can eat!" He looked at me with what I thought was a smile but quickly realized it was a grimace. How dare you...

...come into my establishment looking like You have no honor or pride in your family! I was pissed. How dare he talk to me that way this negro didn't know me. He didn't know my story, and I came in here humbly asking for an opportunity, not a handout. How dare he? So, at this moment, I thought I should cuss this man out or just run out of the store, but before I could gather my thoughts, he spoke again, "Look, young brother, I'm not here to hurt you. I actually love you believe it or not, but you need to comprehend no self-respecting black man will go ask for a job looking like a pauper! You've got to do better. Do you feel me?" I had no clue what he was telling me, so I was honest and said, "No." He went on to explain that our world was created by individuals not interested in me winning or being successful. These folks wanted to see me present and live like a pauper, so every day that I wasn't well dressed, well-read, well-spoken, well learned, and well-traveled, I was feeding into the systematic trap of white supremacy! You could see it on my face...White what? Who is trapped? (I was 11). He then elaborated. You are the son of Kings and slaves, and certain people only want to focus on the slave narrative, and it was my job to tell the story of the king in me. That afternoon, I spent two hours with Mr. Younger, a man I now call uncle! In that time, I learned what it meant to be regal, the importance of confidence, that I would be treated the way I showed up, and most importantly, how I was to show up! I share this with you, young brothers YOU ARE A KING....always show up as one. You will be glad to know I took Mr. Younger's advice and came back the next day and presented myself as a King. At 11, my first real job was sweeping the walk and running errands for Walnut Hill Liquors. My siblings and I didn't miss a meal for the rest of that summer.

Boys Are Outstanding

Let's Talk About Sex

Conversation 17

HEY MAN! Today I want to talk to you about Sex! I want to talk about it because it's super important for you to understand that it's not just something to do. Today's culture is so cavalier about sex. Look up the word cavalier! Everything around us tells us that it's ok to engage in sex. It's become a norm for us. We expect it in relationships even before we really decide if it's someone we want to be with. Magazines, fashion lines, and television commercials, among other things, use sex to sell products and experiences. The truth is sex is dangerous. It's dangerous outside of the way it was supposed to be experienced. No, I'm not about to get all religious on you, but I do need to tell you the truth. Like my friend Hill Harper, the actor, activist, and entrepreneur, said, "Sex is like giving someone the keys to a sports car who has never driven…it can hurt you." Sex is supposed to be enjoyed between two married people. It's how God intended it to be experienced. However, we try to get it whenever and with whomever we can. As men have to be very careful with sex. Sex can cause you to have children you cannot afford to take care of, diseases you cannot get rid of, girls who fall in love with you that you have no intentions of getting into a relationship with, hurt feelings, etc. To keep it real, sex can be scary the more you realize its potential impact on your life. Now I know this is a tough conversation because you are at a stage in your life where the pressure to have sex is unbelievable. Also, your hormones are raging, and you feel like you need to have sex. Trust me, I get it! I was no angel at your age, but as I have gotten older, I have learned that I wasn't being smart at the time with my sexual activity. As a result, I had children that I was not ready to be responsible for. I love my children and would not trade them for the world, but truthfully I was not ready to be a father in any way. I want better for you. I want you to have the right perspective on sex and be able to live your life to the fullest without any regret or hurting others. Be careful with sex. Have an unapologetically amazing day, and remember, man, We just Talkin'! Now, let's see what the fellas have to say about this.

- **From my man Dr. Ryan Ross**

    Man... Yes, I am not going to sit here and lie. I think sex is fantastic. However, because I'm not lying, I'm also going to admit that I think sex is the most dangerous thing a young man can engage in. You see, sex yields an outcome most people, even when they planned for, aren't ready to handle. Sex results in children! Sex is also always followed by one of three things: a soul tie, confrontation, or a positive or negative relationship. In the brief moment you partake in sex, no one ever thinks of these things, especially one of my very best childhood friends. We will call him G. The truth is, G was always the first in our crew to do anything. He was the first to get a debit card, the first with a car, the first to get a full-ride college scholarship offer, and in high school, he was laser-focused on being the first to get the panties, tax some booty, hit the skins, win with the slims... You get it, right? Well, I wish he was laser-focused on something else because his laser-like focus on sex forfeited all his other firsts. What do I mean? I am glad you asked. So, Prom night, in 1997, G decides our crew would have one less virgin. He did everything, including telling the young lady that he loved her. She...

...finally gave in, and the next morning, he proudly let us know that we were boys, and he now was a man! About 6 weeks later, his life would change forever. The young lady was pregnant! "The Man" now quickly wanted to be a boy again...Scholarship gone! He couldn't leave his baby behind, and the school said no thanks when he asked if he could bring his new family. Debit card...Gone. He never had money to do anything again, it seemed like. It was all being saved for the baby, and he wasn't anywhere close to having the funds he needed. The soul tie...he was now connected to a girl he lied to about love, and now she was in his life forever! The positive or negative relationship...BINGO. Negative! Now, all of a sudden, because he wanted sex and to be the man, the young lady was now his barrier. He really blamed her but should have been looking in the Mirror! After all, he loved her, right! One night...one moment...One sexual experience and a whole series of lives were affected forever. I'm not trying to scare you or tell you what you have to do. I'm just talking, and I hope you're listening. I hope you take from this that sex is a serious responsibility, and you should definitely wait until you're ready to engage in all the consequences, opportunities, or outcomes associated with having intercourse.

Who Are Your Friends?

Conversation 18

HEY MAN! Today I want to talk to you about Friendships! The people you call your friends are important. Let me start by saying that we throw the word "friend" around way too easily. Everyone is not your friend. Have you ever looked up the word friend? The definition paints the picture of someone who is very special and close to you, someone who you can tell your darkest secrets and not worry about being judged or your business getting in the streets. So, does everyone you call your friend fit that description? If not, then I call them associates. You can call them what you like, but don't make the mistake of calling them your friend if they fit that description. The truth is that true friends are very hard to find. It's hard to find someone who will put your needs before theirs, someone who will tell you the truth at the risk of your friendship. Someone who is not afraid to tell you no or when you are flat out wrong. Those kinds of people are very rare. Friendships are especially important to your development as a man. As men, we need other men with who we can confide our fears, ask for advice and guidance, learn from, borrow from at times, and have real talks. Honestly, part of what's wrong with the men in our communities is a lack of true male bonding and friendship. There is a lack of real mentors who are not afraid to give it to us straight. Because you are a king and a leader of your family and in your community, it's scary and sometimes embarrassing to confide our vulnerabilities and needs to another man. We feel we may look weak and like a punk. The truth is that we need that. We need that safe place. We need that guidance and male energy to help us at times. So, you see why having a true friend is a valuable thing? True friends help you grow and are good for your mental health. I want you to spend some time thinking about the people you call your friend. You don't have to be mean to those you discover don't fit the definition we looked at earlier, but you do have to be clear about the role they play in your life and the level of access you give them to the inner parts of you. This will help you protect your heart in the long run. It will give you a clear picture of who can qualify to be your friend. Remember, it's super important that your friends are people who cause you to stretch yourself to be better, who you can trust with your secrets and those who you can say anything without fear of it getting out. Have an unapologetically amazing day, and remember, man, We Just Talkin'! Now let's see what the fellas have to say about this.

- **From my man Jermaine Zanders**

    Hey man, we live in a world where social media and reality tv are prevalent in peoples' minds, so it's easy to think that everybody is your friend, but that just 'ain't the truth. People will have hundreds of Facebook friends and even millions of Instagram or Snapchat followers, but these "friends" and "followers" are not REAL friends. Sometimes viewers watch the Real Housewives or Love and Hip-Hop franchises and think that the characters are real and represent real friendships, but these folks are placed together in artificial situations to create ratings. And, people use that word as a casual greeting, "hey friend!" or "Wassup friend?" Honestly, a true friend is ultimately someone you choose to make part of your chosen family. So, when you decide someone is truly your friend, remember that true friendship is built over time, and make sure that s/he is someone you're willing to go to the ends of the earth...

... for because that's exactly what true friends will do. The other mistake we make when it comes to friends is we assume, the more we have, the better off we are. But, my brother, it's just the opposite. Remember that it's quality over quantity when it comes to true friends. I'll keep it 100 with you; my circle of true friends includes about five people who I've known between fifteen to twenty years. These are people who sat by my hospital bed when I was sick. These are people who know I'm not being honest about my true feelings; and will call me to the carpet about it. These are people who will not allow me to give up on myself because they're able to see greatness in me when I can't see it for myself. You see, real friends are just that – REAL. So, remember to keep that circle of friends tight because these are the people who will always stand by you and have your back.

Yo Momma!....
That's Right I Said It

Conversation 19

HEY MAN, today I want to talk to you about your Mother. Yes, YO MAMA! Your mother is arguably the most important person in your life. This is the person that gives you life, that carries you before you are probably formed, and the person who teaches you how to love and care for yourself and others. Sometimes relationships with your mothers can be complicated and tricky. Only because as much as she is equipped to teach you to nurture and bring you into this life, inherently, you still need a man to show you how to be a man. Therefore, some of your rebellious behavior towards your mother can be attributed to the fact that you inherently crave a man's respect and approval. There are certain things that only a man's advice can reach or touch and your spirit. However, back to your mother. Love her and protect her with all your heart. Even if the relationship is strained at times, know that you would not feel what you feel or be where you are if it wasn't for her sacrifice of giving you birth. I underestimated the power of this relationship until my mother died. Afterward, I realized that I didn't say I love you enough, spend enough time with her, or value her input in my life as much. Now that she is gone, I know that there is a hole that only a mother can fill in my soul. So please remember to respect your mother and let her know how much you appreciate what she has done for you if it's only that she gave you life. Remember, man, We Just Talkin'! Now let's see what the fellas have to say about this.

- **From my man Jermaine Zanders**

    Hey man, no subject in the world will spark a fight with someone quicker than talking about their momma. Let me tell you, can't nobody tell me about my momma; you can't say one single, solitary word about the woman who gave me life, nurtured me, cared for me, supported me, and pushed me to be my best self. Our mothers are so special because there is no love like her love. Now, I recognize that every mother-son relationship is not necessarily positive, but regardless of how you feel about her, always remember that she gave you life; she shared her body and soul with you, typically for nine months. For that, you should always be grateful because she got you here! Let that example and that fact always allow you to look upon your mother with love. I'll be honest, there are some things I wish my mother would have done differently while I was growing up, but now as an adult, I realize she did the best she knew how to do at that time. I had to learn that my mother, like the rest of us, is human, so I am grateful that I have the mother I have, she might not be perfect, but she was the perfect mother for me. Know that because of your momma, you have the opportunity to be great, so take advantage of it and work each day to make "yo mama proud!"

Winning.....Without Charlie Sheen Tiger Blood

Conversation 20

HEY MAN, today I want to talk to you about Winning. What do you think about when the word "winning" is said? Do you automatically think about sports, or do you think of other ways of winning that have nothing to do with sports? What if I told you that you could either win or lose in life. What would that mean to you? It's true, though! For example, if you are doing well in school, moving towards your goal of graduation, work, or college successfully, then you are considered to be winning! But, if you are getting in trouble all the time, suspended, expelled, and missing a lot of school, then you are definitely losing. The way to ensure that you are always on a winning path, even if you take a few L's, is to always be moving forward toward your goals. There will be times where it will seem like you are not making any real progress, but I have found that as long as you are doing your best to be your best, you eventually get to where you want to be. You have to be willing to do what you have to do to eventually do what you want to do. Ya dig? Hey, the bottom line is that you are in control of how much you win or lose. It's a matter of perspective and effort. Remember, man, We Just Talkin'! Now, let's see what the fellas have to say about this!

- **From my man Dionizio Fisher**

    I'm happy to talk to you about my perception of the word "winning." When I think about winning, what first comes to mind has more to do with life, in general, more than any particular sport or competition. I believe that it is true that most people can be classified as being in a state of either winning or a state of losing, but I don't necessarily think that that state should be defined by that person's current position in life. What I mean is, I believe that you can be defined as winning or losing, not because of how much money you have or how much property you own, but rather because of where you are mentally and spiritually in your life. So, for example, if you are rich but you aren't humble, if you don't have love for your family or your community, and your family and community don't have real love for you; or if you're a great athlete, but you abuse your wife and kids through violence, or you abuse yourself with drug and addiction, then to me, you are losing. Now, on the other hand, if you are poor, or struggling every day to pay your bills, but you still put all of your efforts into making sure your kids grow up educated, self-reliant, and honest; or if you love your family and your community, and you always try to be a better person, no matter what challenges that you face on a daily, then to me you're winning. I use those 2 extreme scenarios only to point out that there can be many different interpretations of winning or losing, but for me, a lot of it has more to do with your state of mind and your determination to be a better person that makes you a winner in my book. Even when you fall on your face, as long as you get back up and back in the race, even if you come in last, you're still a winner because you didn't quit.

- **From my man Jonathan McMillan**

    It's been my experience that winning can always be experienced through an attitude of gratitude. By learning to have and express genuine gratitude for every opportunity, experience, and relationship, a dynamic shift happens in a person's thinking, behavior, and character. Therefore you're in a constant state of winning. Grateful people are more productive members of their households, communities, workplaces, and the world at large. Grateful people, by extension, possess mindsets and personalities that are more positive than others who are don't understand or neglect the power of gratitude. Allow me to share a short story about how this concept worked in my life. A few years ago, I was experiencing some of the biggest challenges I had ever faced in my life up to that point.

    I had lost my job; my wife was six months pregnant, and I had been accused of committing a crime of which I was innocent and facing some major prison time. I was in a deep depression and felt hopeless because I saw no "win" anywhere on my horizon. I moped around the house and was withdrawing from everyone around me. Then one day, after getting sick of my attitude, my wife checked me on my self-pity. She reminded me of all of the good things I had going for me and how I should take advantage of them now before I lost them too by neglecting them.

I immediately shifted my focus and began to be intentional about recognizing all that I had in my life, which benefited me. I began to challenge myself to intentionally recognize and acknowledge at least 17 unique things a day for which I could and should be grateful. I noted everything from the warmth of the sun on my skin on a hot day to the odor of the garbage because both sensations were evidence that I was alive and able to experience life in its wholeness. Eventually, I was able to even be grateful for the challenges I was going through because the valuable lessons they were teaching me made me wiser and, therefore, more valuable. The more I looked for opportunities to be grateful, the more opportunities presented themselves to me. Before long, I was back in a healthy, happy state of mind and able to be productive economically and socially. I met some of the best people in the world who made a practice of winning daily and allowed me to be on their team. The bottom line, winning is an attitude of gratitude. And developing and practicing the habit and skill of being sincerely grateful powerfully attracts more people and things into your life to be thankful for, especially opportunities and experiences, and puts you in a position to constantly win!

BOYS ARE BRILLIANT

Failure

Conversation 21

HEY MAN, today I want to talk to you about Failure! I know it's not a word many want to hear or admit to. Failure is usually associated with not getting something done, but it doesn't have to be all bad. With the right perspective, failure can be better than success sometimes. When you are successful, there are a few things that you learn. When you experience failure, you can learn a lot! As you are trying to get it right, you try various ways to get it done, so by default, you go through various variations of what you are trying to get right. You get exposed to more options when you fail. Also, failure, at a basic level, shows you what doesn't work! While it doesn't always feel good, I've learned to appreciate failure when it happens. Now that doesn't mean I don't get upset or hurt when it happens because I do! I'm saying that I now know that I have an optional way to look at it. A way that's positive and one that helps me grow! Remember, man, We Just Talkin'! Now let's see what the fellas have to say about this.

- **From my man Dionizio Fisher**

    Failure is just as tough as you described: It's hard, it can make you feel defeated and want to give up, and it can make you question who you are as a person and a man. In fact, for some people, it might seem like they try and try their hardest to win but still come up short every time. For people who grew up on the same side of the tracks as I did, it would seem like failure was more of the norm than the exception. But it's been my experience that those same people who have had the toughest upbringings and suffered the most defeats, but never quit or give up, no matter how many times they fail, those are usually the most well rounded and determined people I have come to know in my life. In my opinion, you can often fail and even spectacularly, but you will never be an actual failure until the day you decide to give up or quit trying. For example, in Rocky, Rocky Balboa losses his fight with Apollo Creed, but most everyone remembers it as a victory because round after round, hit after hit, punch after punch, Rocky never gives up, he never backs down, and he keeps fighting until the final bell. He failed to win the fight, but he won in life just the same.

- **From my man Jonathan McMillan**

    There's a saying that goes something like this; "Most people never become more than what they currently are." and that's because most of us have an irrational fear of failure. Whether it be some type of change, big or small, leaving your comfort zone and taking on new challenges, people fear the possibility of failure. But you cannot let these fears override your desire for what you know is best for you and your family. In the film After Earth, Will Smith's character stated, "The only place that fear can exist is in our thoughts of the future. It is a product of our...

...imagination, causing us to fear things that do not at present and may not ever exist. That is near insanity. Do not misunderstand me. Danger is very real - but fear is a choice." What that soliloquy illustrates is the power of emotionalizing. That is the act of imagining how it will feel when you achieve or don't achieve your goal. For most people, fear is an emotion that motivates them to create and achieve goals so insignificant they are practically subconscious. The fear of getting fired or being homeless is precisely what keeps them diligently showing up to an unsatisfying job where they perform just well enough not to get fired. Paying bills, rent, and putting food on the table - just surviving - becomes the goal. Emotionalizing what not surviving feels like is what keeps them going. Emotionalizing what it feels like to fail is what keeps most people from ever trying anything new or taking any risks. Whether it be new foods or new careers. We turn up our noses and scowl our faces at the mere thought of trying foods that are untested but different. They could be disgusting! But they also could be delicious! What if you focused the power of emotionalizing not on failure but on something good like achievements and successes? How much more would you accomplish if you emotionalized pride? How much bigger and significant would the goals you set be? Chances are they would be better than average. Especially if you took on the perspective that failure isn't necessarily bad to experience. There is a difference between failing and being a failure. Mistakes are just proof of effort, and failures are great learning opportunities. Success comes from changing your perception of failures into lessons that make you wiser and more valuable. When things go wrong, you only become a failure if you don't take time to examine what you could have done differently and re-examine your strategy or if you give up.

- **From my man Sean Bell**

    Failure is inevitable and necessary for growth and success. I repeat, failure is inevitable and necessary for growth and success. In the type of work I do, I see young men who put undue pressure on themselves because they will not allow themselves to fail. This is a daunting task because we fail daily. We fail to get up the first time our alarm goes off, or we fail to catch the train as we run urgently to get to our destination. These failures are easy to swallow because the consequences are not always colossal, and for some reason, we have told ourselves that we can be successful the next time. What if we looked at all failures in the same way despite the consequence? It takes a different thought pattern, but I believe it can be done. I know failure fairly well. A few years ago, I was kicked out of my doctoral program because I did not finish in time as I took time off without technically withdrawing from the program. This failure has not only impacted me financially but emotionally. I did not realize that I was depressed and carried so much guilt because I did...

...not finish this program. I was also extremely embarrassed as many of my friends and family were completing their doctorates, and I had to take a deep gulp every time I attended a graduation ceremony or witnessed a post on social media. It is still uncomfortable for me, depending on the day.

However, depression and embarrassment do not make the situation fade away. In fact, these things make matters worse. It wasn't until I changed my perspective that I understood that I could still strive. I started my own business, obtained my MBA, and became a Certified Life Coach. I realized that I was successful at many things and that I would not dwell on the one thing that I did not accomplish. I will fail again, and I will be successful right after that. You will fail again, and you will be successful. It's inevitable! Don't be afraid to fail! Trust that you can go through it and do well on the other side of it. Learn from it and move on, no matter how long it takes you.

"Gentlemen, I really hope you enjoyed reading these conversations as much as we enjoyed writing them. My hope is that you reflected on each conversation and thought about how to engage with these different areas of your life when they come up. It's not easy being a man all the time, but when we get it right, it's worth every moment of the responsibility that's been placed on us. Those of us who were a part of bringing this book to life appreciate the experiences that allowed us to talk to you about them. One day, you'll be in a position to do the same for other young men who you don't even know yet. That's the beauty of growth. It makes you better for others around you also! Until next time, be cool and remember

WE JUST TALKIN'"

With Love and Respect, your man Dedrick Sims